D1424681

NAVIGATING STEVENSON

This book is due for return on or before the last date shown below.

Don Gresswell Ltd., London, N.21   Cat. No. 1208   DG 02242/71

Elaine Greig · James Lawson · Catherine Moriarty

Navigating Stevenson

Digital Artworks by Sara Gadd

Scottish National Portrait Gallery
Edinburgh · 2003

Published by the Trustees of the National Galleries
of Scotland to accompany the exhibition *Navigating Stevenson:
Digital Artworks by Sara Gadd* held at the Scottish National Portrait
Gallery, Edinburgh from 31 January to 11 May 2003 and on tour to
Callendar House, Falkirk; Collins Gallery, University of Strathclyde;
and Brighton Museum and Art Gallery

ISBN 1 903278 41 4

Designed and typeset in New Caledonia by Dalrymple
Printed in Belgium by Snoeck-Ducaju & Zoon

Contents

Foreword

Robert Louis Stevenson's life and writing continue to fascinate, receiving seemingly constant reassessment from literary critics and biographers. However, the visual legacy of Stevenson's travels has only rarely been explored and we are proud to be one of a number of venues staging this innovative exhibition of digital artwork by Sara Gadd. She offers a way of exploring virtually Stevenson's past that is both cerebral and exciting.

The exhibition is the product of a collaboration involving amongst others the Scottish Arts Council, Napier University and The Writers' Museum in Edinburgh. We would like to acknowledge all our co-partners for their enthusiasm for the project and generous support. We would also like to thank staff at the National Galleries of Scotland for all their efforts, including Duncan Forbes who curated the exhibition. Finally, special thanks to Sara Gadd for her commitment to the exhibition and to the writers who contributed so willingly to the catalogue.

SIR TIMOTHY CLIFFORD
Director-General, National Galleries of Scotland

JAMES HOLLOWAY
Director, Scottish National Portrait Gallery

Acknowledgements

I would like to thank the following organisations for their contribution and support to this project: The Writers' Museum, Edinburgh; the Scottish National Portrait Gallery, Edinburgh; Callendar House, Falkirk; Brighton Museum and Art Gallery and the Collins Gallery, University of Strathclyde, Glasgow. I also wish to thank the Woo Foundation for their award and to Spectrum Photographic for their continual professional guidance and support with printing and production of the artwork.

In addition, I would like to convey special thanks to the following individuals without whom this project would not have been possible: Elaine Greig, Curator, The Writers' Museum, Edinburgh, for her patience and guidance and for allowing me access to the Robert Louis Stevenson collection and also for her essay; Duncan Forbes, Senior Curator of Photography, at the Scottish National Portrait Gallery for his support of the project, and to Dr Catherine Moriarty, Curator, Design Council Archive, University of Brighton and James Lawson, Lecturer, Department of Architecture, University of Edinburgh for their insightful essays about this new work.

Also, my thanks to Huw Davies, Head of the School of Design and Media Arts and the academic staff for my selection as Fellow in Photography and Digital Imaging and to Maike Beveridge for continual administrative support; Duncan Hepburn, Lecturer, School of Design and Media Arts, Napier University and technical staff for helping me through the complex process of 3D computer design work and Matthew Abbott, freelance designer. And finally, thanks to David Leeming of The Speculative Society, University of Edinburgh.

SARA GADD

Introduction

DUNCAN FORBES

In June 1888, the San Francisco schooner, *Casco,* set its compass for the South Seas with Robert Louis Stevenson and his family entourage on board. The voyage would prove a turning point in the writer's life, repairing his shattered health, forcing a conclusive distance from literary circles in Britain, and offering practical experience of the ethic of adventure that lay at the heart of his imaginative vision. Stevenson was the most sophisticated of Victorian travellers, coming to understand through his energetic and serious-minded engagement with the Polynesian people the full horror, and wonder, of the colonial encounter. During his six years in the Pacific islands, Stevenson's profound relief at nullifying the strictures of his Scottish upbringing also sparked his most perceptive writing on his native land.

It is this context of cultural exchange – the fact, according to Edward Said, that 'partly because of empire, all cultures are involved in one another' – that underpins the logic of this exhibition and its accompanying publication.[1] Throughout much of his life Stevenson was self-avowedly an exile, feeding his talent by prolonged journeying with what another critic has described as the 'stimulus of dislocation'.[2] It would be simple to posit this as a romantic impulse, inserting the author into a story of empire that also features the Scots missionary and commercial trader, each arriving on the shores of Polynesia's complex archipelago in pursuit of quick profit or easy conversion. However, Stevenson's experience of Samoa fired a deeper curiosity, and was attended by greater generosity, than this suggests. It is part of the interest of his presence in the South Seas that he constantly pushed at the boundaries of the literary conventions and cultural suppositions that took him there. Stevenson opposed what he described as the 'sugar candy sham epic' of the exotic travelogue;[3] he became rapidly attuned to – as well as actively engaged in combating – the worst excesses that accompanied the colonists' jostling for power. The writer came to assume a sense of responsibility for Samoa and hoped, by challenging and overturning pernicious stereotypes, to encourage a similar commitment amongst his readership at home.[4]

Stevenson's desire to record and communicate his experiences survives for us today in the form of his writing (letters, essays and fiction), family photographs, and a number of treasured personal possessions now housed in museums around the world. It is these documents and objects that Sara Gadd draws on in her imaginative re-creation of Stevenson's stay in the Pacific. Her reworking and repositioning of artefacts digitally within the 'spaces' created by the computer draws special attention to the visual legacy of Stevenson's travels, and especially the albums of photographs now stored in The Writers' Museum in Edinburgh. These often anonymous images, many taken by members of Stevenson's family, were intended as stimulating souvenirs, and perhaps also as illustrations for a projected book about the South Seas. They point to the dense interdependence of photography and tourism during the nineteenth century, as an apparently reliable record of sights previously unseen, as well as an incitement to others to explore the scenery of empire.[5] If, as Nancy Armstrong has recently argued, there is a peculiarly close relationship between literary description and photography during this period, then the regime of the visual – and these photographs in particular – may have been more important to Stevenson's writing than has previously been acknowledged.[6]

The earliest known photographs of Samoa date from the 1860s, produced by an ad hoc assemblage of amateurs, missionaries and imperial officials. Commercial photographers began to appear in the islands from the mid-1880s, catering in a more systematic way for the burgeoning tourist trade.[7] As historians have recently emphasised, photography was an important mechanism of imperial domination, offering knowledge of colonial territories and peoples which, subject to systems of classification, could then be used to justify biological or cultural theories of Western superiority. It may be impossible to disassociate the Stevenson photographs from these broader uses of photography, but they also embody motivations and sources of identification that are at once more involved and prosaic. The albums hover precariously between different kinds of record: the Victorian travelogue, the family portrait and the story of a famous life. They also attest to the powerful contemporary will to archive: to document, to gather, to force a specious unity on new, impossibly diverse fields of knowledge and experience.[8] There is a sense in which these photographs provide both the most reliable, and most fantastic, traces of Stevenson's life in the South Seas.

It is these historical problems that inform Sara Gadd's images, and it is to these issues that they ask us to refer. But as the essays in this catalogue point out, her digital artworks are also dependent on a fundamental transformation of archival objects, a reordering of the sources that inform our knowledge of Stevenson's experience of Polynesia and its people. Using computer software, photographs become simulations; their evidential, indexical (that is, in some sense, direct) link to the world is creatively transformed. Objects are freed from their museum environments, disembodied, recombined and given new meaning in virtual spaces. To what extent this represents a liberation of visual knowledge from the prison house of the physical archive is one of the questions this exhibition sets out to explore. It offers Sara Gadd striking aesthetic possibilities – she generates a 'synthetic realism' of remarkable formal complexity.[9] At the same time, as Catherine Moriarty argues here, digital replication generates anxiety, forcing us to abandon ingrained notions of authenticity, compelling us no longer to mistake images for the things they represent. A digital future asks us all to be less passive in the face of visual information, in the present, but also from the past.

Sara Gadd's 'inauthentic' images guide us back to Stevenson, the South Seas and a reconsideration of the objects he left behind. They ask us to rethink the role of the archive in an era of quickening technological change. As she has discovered, Stevenson's story is irresistible, for the histories of empire and migration that shaped him are situated at the very heart of Scottish – and British – culture.

1. *Culture and Imperialism*, London, 1994, p.xxix.

2. J.C. Furnas, 'Stevenson and exile', in Jenni Calder (ed.), *Stevenson and Victorian Scotland*, Edinburgh, 1981, p.132.

3. Stevenson to Sidney Colvin, Vailima, 28 September 1891, in *The Letters of Robert Louis Stevenson*, Bradford A. Booth and Ernest Mehew (eds.), 8 vols., New Haven and London, 1994–5, vol.7, p.161.

4. This is not, however, to argue that Stevenson was in any sense a radical or committed to the end of British involvement in empire. For a discussion of what he argues was Stevenson's essentially patrician Tory politics, see Christopher Harvie, 'The Politics of Stevenson', in *Stevenson and Victorian Scotland*, pp.107–25.

5. For a discussion of the issues raised here, see Peter D. Osborne, *Travelling Light: Photography, Travel and Visual Culture*, Manchester, 2000.

6. Nancy Armstrong, *Fiction in the Age of Photography: the Legacy of British Realism*, Cambridge, Massachusetts, and London, 1999.

7. Casey Blanton (ed.), *Picturing Paradise: Colonial Photography of Samoa, 1875 to 1925*, Southeast Museum of Photography, Daytona, 1995.

8. For a fascinating discussion of the historical questions touched on here see Thomas Richards, *The Imperial Archive: Knowledge and the Fantasy of Empire*, London, 1993.

9. The phrase is that of Lev Manovich, in his *The Language of New Media*, Cambridge, Massachusetts, 2001. This book is a useful introduction to issues raised by electronic literature and art.

Absolute Balm for the Weary

ELAINE GREIG

This climate; these voyagings; these landfalls at dawn; new islands peaking from the morning bank; new, forested harbours; new passing alarms of squalls and surf; new, interests of gentle natives – the whole tale of my life is better to me than any poem.[1]

Recognised all over the world as the author of *Treasure Island, Kidnapped* and *The Strange Case of Dr Jekyll and Mr Hyde,* the name Robert Louis Stevenson conjures up images of pirates, potions, excitement and adventure. Perhaps less well known, but just as compelling, is the real life story of Stevenson.

He was born in Edinburgh on 13 November 1850, the only child of Thomas Stevenson, one of the illustrious family of harbour and lighthouse engineers, and his wife Margaret, a daughter of the Reverend Dr Lewis Balfour of Colinton. Stevenson grew up in comparative comfort, despite the poor health that affected him all his life. Able to attend formal schooling for only brief periods, he spent much time in 'the land of counterpane', marching his soldiers over the quilt, enacting dramas with his toy theatre, and listening to stories from the Bible and from Scottish history. The character of Scotland and Edinburgh, past and present, fired his imagination and influenced his life and work. In a letter to his mother he wrote: 'I wish that life was an opera. I should like to *live* in one.'[2]

It had always been assumed that the young Stevenson would follow family tradition and become a civil engineer, but although he showed promise in this field, it was not what he aspired to do. After overcoming opposition from his parents, he embarked upon a career as a writer, becoming well known for his many novels, essays, travel books and poetry.

Travel was something Stevenson always enjoyed. While in France in 1876 he met and fell in love with Fanny Osbourne, an American with two children who was separated from her husband. Stevenson followed her to California, a hazardous journey by ship and train of over three weeks, and they were married in San Francisco in May 1880. His poor health forced him to continue to search for a more congenial climate and he and Fanny spent time in various locations in Scotland, England and mainland Europe.

In 1887, following the death of his father, Stevenson – with his wife, mother and stepson, Lloyd – left Edinburgh for the last time and set sail for America where they spent the winter at a sanatorium at Saranac in the Adirondack Mountains of upper New York State. There they planned a trip to the South Seas and Fanny was sent on ahead to San Francisco to find a suitable ship to take them on this new adventure. Stevenson wrote of his proposed travels in a letter to his friend Lady Taylor:

We sail from San Francisco in the schooner yacht 'Casco', for a seven months' cruise in the South Seas ... this is an old dream of mine which actually seems to be coming true ... from poking in a sick-room all winter to the deck of one's own ship, is indeed a heavenly change.[3]

Stevenson had wished to travel to the islands of the South Pacific since 1875, when an 'awfully nice man', William Seed, a New Zealand civil servant, visited the family home in Edinburgh. Stevenson wrote to his friend and confidante, Mrs Frances Sitwell: 'Telling us all about the South Sea Islands till I was sick with desire to go there; beautiful places, green forever; perfect climate ... Navigator's Islands [Samoa] is the place; absolute balm for the weary.'[4] Between 1888 and 1890, Stevenson undertook three cruises among the islands of the South Pacific.

On 28 June 1888, accompanied by Fanny, Lloyd and his mother, he travelled on board the *Casco* to the Marquesas Islands, the Paumotus Islands (now Tuamotus), Tahiti and Hawaii. The *Casco* was called *Pahi Muni* (the *Silver Ship*) by the people of Fakarava, 'her fine lines, tall spars, and snowy decks, the crimson fittings of the saloon, and the white, the gilt, and the repeating mirrors of the tiny cabin, brought us a hundred visitors.'[5] In the relaxed lifestyle he enjoyed in the South Seas he seemed finally to have escaped the constraints of poor health and the conventions of Victorian Britain. His wife, Fanny, wrote to their close friend, Sidney Colvin: 'he has gained health and strength every day. He takes sea baths, and even swims, and lives almost entirely in the open air as nearly without clothes as possible, a simple pyjama suit of striped light

flannel his only dress.'[6]

They arrived at Honolulu on 24 January 1889 and were met by Fanny's daughter, Belle, her husband, Joe Strong, and eight-year-old son, Austin. Stevenson rented a house at Waikiki, where he finished *The Master of Ballantrae*, and he became a popular addition to Hawaiian society and a close friend of King Kalakaua and other members of the Hawaiian royal family. Stevenson wrote to Sidney Colvin, in April 1889: *We are not coming home for another year. I cannot but hope it may continue the vast improvement of my health...and we have all a taste for this wandering and dangerous life...I cannot say why I like the sea; no man is more cynically and constantly alive to its perils; I regard it as the highest form of gambling; and yet I love the sea as much as I hate gambling. Fine, clean emotions; a world all and always beautiful; air better than wine; interest unflagging; there is upon the whole no better life.*[7]

On 24 June 1889, Stevenson, with Fanny, Lloyd and Joe, left Hawaii on board the *Equator* to cruise to the Gilbert Islands (now Kiribati) and Samoa. According to the local paper: *The object of Mr Stevenson undertaking this adventurous voyage, is to become acquainted more fully with the uncivilised habits of South Sea Islanders; and the public may expect that his next book will be largely devoted to these experiences and scenes from islands little known to the reading world.*[8]

The earlier cruise, on the *Casco*,

had involved taking a typewriter and photographic equipment with which to document their travels. Now Stevenson planned to develop his growing affinity with island life with a proposed illustrated work, detailing the history and anthropology of the whole area, to be called *The South Seas*. In June he wrote to Colvin about this project: 'By the time I am done with this cruise I shall have the material for a very singular book of travels: masses of strange stories and characters, cannibals, pirates, ancient legends, old Polynesian poetry; never was so generous a farrago.'[9]

Stevenson intended to write more than just a personal travelogue. During the cruises he kept a journal noting meetings with local chiefs, missionaries, reformed cannibals, traders and fortune-hunters: 'The Pacific is a strange place; the nineteenth century only exists there in spots; all round, it is a no man's land of the ages, a stir-about of epochs and races, barbarisms and civilisations, virtues and crimes.'[10]

The photographs from Stevenson's travels are now kept by The Writers' Museum in Edinburgh. There are four albums, one for each of the cruises (on board the *Casco*, *Equator*, and SS *Janet Nicoll*) and one covering the author's life on Samoa. The photographs are varied, ranging from amateur snapshots – taken using Lloyd Osbourne's button-hole camera – to good quality prints produced by commercial photogra-

phers based in Tahiti and Honolulu. They document daily life in the islands, people befriended by Stevenson as well as buildings, costume, landscape, events and some shots taken indoors and at night. Stevenson probably intended some of the images to illustrate his projected book on the South Seas. Together, as albums, they now construct a complex and engaging visual travelogue.

Although Stevenson set out his plans for the book, the material he collected was never published in such a comprehensive form. Much of what he wrote was not considered personal enough by editors, friends or public. The whole subject, after all, was alien to most readers. Perhaps a series of newsy letters about his travels might have pleased more people, including his wife, but Stevenson wanted to be factual. In this respect he was ahead of his time. He was conscious of a vanishing way of life. Although struck by the beauty of the islands, he was very aware of cultural contrasts and, due to the impact of colonialism, the gradual extinction of the customs and traditions of the islanders. Writing in his book, published posthumously Stevenson wrote: 'ten years more, and the old society will have entirely vanished'.[11]

Stevenson was uncomfortable with the concept of colonialism; the imposition of one culture upon another, and he saw similarities to the demise of the clan system in the Highlands of Scotland, also based on extended loyalty to family and name. His South Seas inspired novels, particularly *The Beach of Falesa* and *The Ebb-Tide*, reflect this cultural cauldron.

On 7 December 1889, the *Equator* arrived at Apia, the capital and port of Upolu, the largest of the Samoan Islands. As Stevenson's health had greatly improved in the climate of the South Seas, he finally decided to settle in Samoa, purchasing an estate of over 400 acres which the family called Vailima (meaning the place of five waters). He described the effect of the climate, in a letter, to Lady Taylor: 'here I have some real health, I can walk, I can ride, I can stand some exposure, I am up with the sun, I have a real enjoyment of the world and of myself.'[12]

Intending to travel back to Britain to make arrangements for permanent residence, Stevenson set out for Australia, but on reaching Sydney he took ill. He returned to Samoa, via Auckland, on board the *SS Janet Nicoll*. The cramped life on board ship did not suit Fanny, who was prone to seasickness, but Stevenson thrived: 'so long as I cruise in the South Seas, I shall be well and happy … so soon as I cease from cruising, the nerves are strained, the decline commences, and I steer slowly but surely back to bedward.'[13]

After viewing the progress on the construction of their new home, Stevenson, Fanny and Lloyd set off on 1 May on board the *SS Janet Nicoll*, sailing east as far as Penrhyn Island before returning west through the Ellice Islands to revisit the Gilbert Islands, and on to New Caledonia, where they arrived on 26 July 1890. While Lloyd travelled to Britain to settle their affairs, Stevenson and Fanny returned to Samoa in September on the *SS Lübeck*, where they supervised the completion of their new home.

By October 1892, Stevenson was the owner of a large house and head of a household of five relatives and thirteen staff. Aware of his position of power and responsibility, he became increasingly involved in the politics of the islands, defending the needs and traditions of the islanders against the impact of colonialism and threats of civil war. In 1891, he wrote to Colvin: *How am I to describe my life these last few days? I have been wholly swallowed up in politics; a wretched business, with fine elements of farce in it too … a mass of fudge and fun, which would have driven me crazy ten years ago and now makes me smile.*[14]

Since the Berlin Treaty of 1889, Samoa had been administered jointly by Germany, Britain and the US, with a 'king' as nominal head. Civil war broke out in July 1893 between the rival claimants: the German-backed Malietoa Laupepa, and Mata'afa Iosefo who received some support from Britain and America was also favoured by Stevenson. Mata'afa was defeated in July 1893 and exiled. Stevenson secured the release of the other chiefs and, as a token of their gratitude, they built a road leading to Vailima. A feast was given in celebration of the completion of 'The Road of the Loving Heart' on 7 October 1894.

The tense political situation together with financial pressure and worry over the health of Fanny and other members of the household – which was in contrast to his own reasonable health – caused him great concern. Also, the realisation had dawned that he would never, indeed could never, return to Scotland, In letters written during the last two years of his life he became more and more gloomy about the future and frequently referred to his death. 'Vailima … [is] beautiful and my home and tomb that is to be; though it's a wrench not to be planted in Scotland.'[15]

Robert Louis Stevenson died of a brain haemorrhage on 3 December 1894 and was buried on Mount Vaea overlooking Vailima. He left behind seven unfinished books – and the myth of a famous writer who died young in a romantic part of the world.

1. Letter to James Payn, from Honolulu, 13 June 1889, vol.6, p.317.

2. Letter to Margaret Stevenson, from Frankfurt, 6 August 1872, vol.1, p.243.

3. Letter to Lady Taylor, from Manasquan, c. 15 May 1888, vol.6, p.184.

4. Letter to Frances Sitwell, from Edinburgh, c. 21 June 1875, vol.2, p.145.

5. Robert Louis Stevenson, In the South Seas, London, 1998, p.11.

6. Letter from Fanny Stevenson to Sidney Colvin, Tautira, Tahiti, 4 December 1888, vol.6, p.227.

7. Letter to Sidney Colvin, from Honolulu, 2 April 1889, vol.6, p.276.

8. Daily Pacific Commercial Advertiser, 24 June 1889.

9. Letter to Sidney Colvin, from Honolulu, early June 1889, vol.6, p.312.

10. Letter to Sidney Colvin, from Honolulu, early June 1889, vol.6, p.312.

11. Robert Louis Stevenson, In the South Seas, London, 1998, p.156.

12. Letter to Lady Taylor, from Apia, Samoa, 20 January 1890, vol.6, p.352.

13. Letter to Sidney Colvin, at sea, 30 April 1890, vol.6, p.388.

14. Letter to Sidney Colvin, from Vailima, 13 October 1891, vol.7, p.163.

15. Letter to Sidney Colvin, from Vailima, 4 September 1893, vol.8, p.159.

Note: All letters quoted, except for notes 5, 8, & 11 are from Robert Louis Stevenson, The Letters of Robert Louis Stevenson, Bradford A. Booth and Ernest Mehew, 8 vols., New Haven and London, 1994–5.

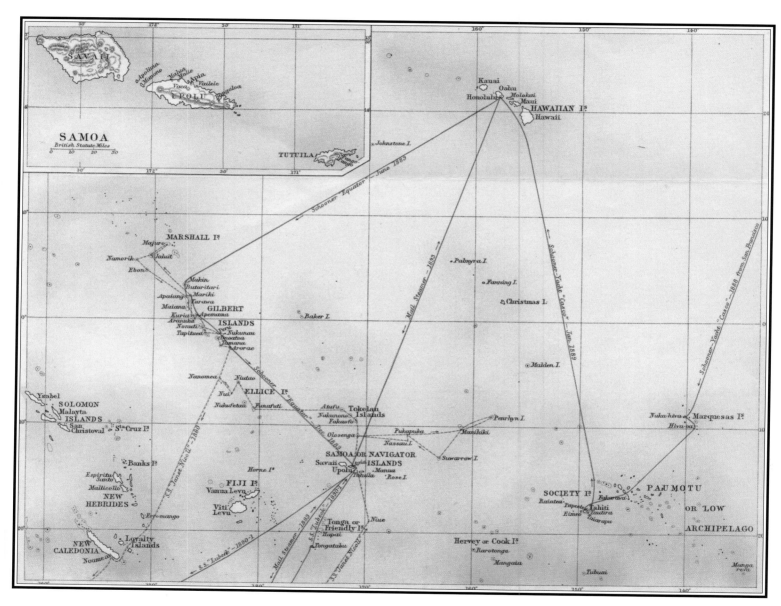

Stevenson's Travels in the South Seas

Navigating Stevenson

On Board the Yacht, *Casco*, Stevenson Awaits the Arrival of Kooamua, Chief of Hatiheu, a Civilised Cannibal and the Last Eater of Long-pig

In June 1888, Stevenson left San Franciso on board the *Casco*, arriving in the Marquesas Islands some three weeks later. In a letter to a friend, the writer noted that it was 'all a swindle: I chose these isles as having the most beastly population, and they are far better, and far more civilised than we'. Stevenson's engagement with indigenous cultures is a feature of his time in the Pacific. Here, the inclusion of his dinner plates, now stored in The Writers' Museum in Edinburgh, refers to Stevenson's thoughts on the tradition of cannibalism and the wider meanings of the word 'civilisation' in the context of his experience of the South Seas.

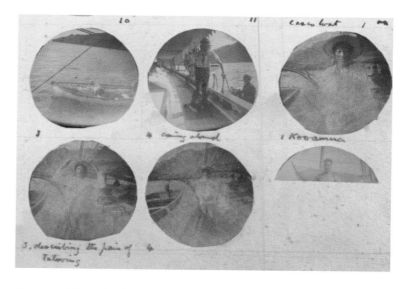

Coming Aboard, The Marquesas, at Anaho Bay
Casco Album, The Writers' Museum, Edinburgh

2   Five Months in Hawaii

In January 1889, the Stevenson party was formally introduced to the King of Hawaii, Kalakaua. The king tried unsuccessfully over the following months to persuade the author to settle permanently in Honolulu. The interior of the king's boathouse provided a splendid venue in which to wine and dine. Stevenson's boots, now kept by The Writers' Museum, suggest both the reality of his extended stay, and also the fact that he was not entirely 'at home' on the island. During his time in Hawaii, Stevenson was always planning his next journey, at one point travelling to visit the islands' leper colony.

Feast Given by HM King Kalakaua of the Hawaiian Islands
to R.L. Stevenson and Party at Waikiki
Casco Album, The Writers' Museum, Edinburgh

3 The Drunken Thrones of the King and Queen of Butaritari

The *Equator* arrived in Butaritari in July 1889 and the Stevensons took up residence with an Hawaiian missionary. The island was in festive mood after its king had lifted a traditional ban on alcohol. The image refers to the mass drunkenness that gripped the island (and includes a wine glass used by Stevenson at Vailima). Stevenson became involved in reimposing the *tapu* – or ban – on alcohol in defiance of the king and white traders who had been supplying a constant stream of gin, beer and brandy. Two weeks later, the debauchery was ended, and the king and queen once again sat aloft on their thrones.

The Church with Raised Thrones in which the King and Queen Sit in State, Butaritari, Gilbert Islands
Equator Album, The Writers' Museum, Edinburgh

4 Catching Fish off the Bowsprit of the Schooner, *Equator*

In June 1889, the *Equator* sailed from Honolulu through the Gilbert Islands towards Samoa. Stevenson loved the sea for the adventure it promised and the benefits it offered his health – the original album photograph provides an unusual snapshot of his energetic involvement in fishing. Stevenson's fish hooks from The Writers' Museum are incorporated into the digital image. They are fashioned from mother of pearl and tortoiseshell, wound with a natural binding and intricately carved.

Spearing Fish off the Bowsprit around the Kingsmill Islands
Equator Album, The Writers' Museum, Edinburgh

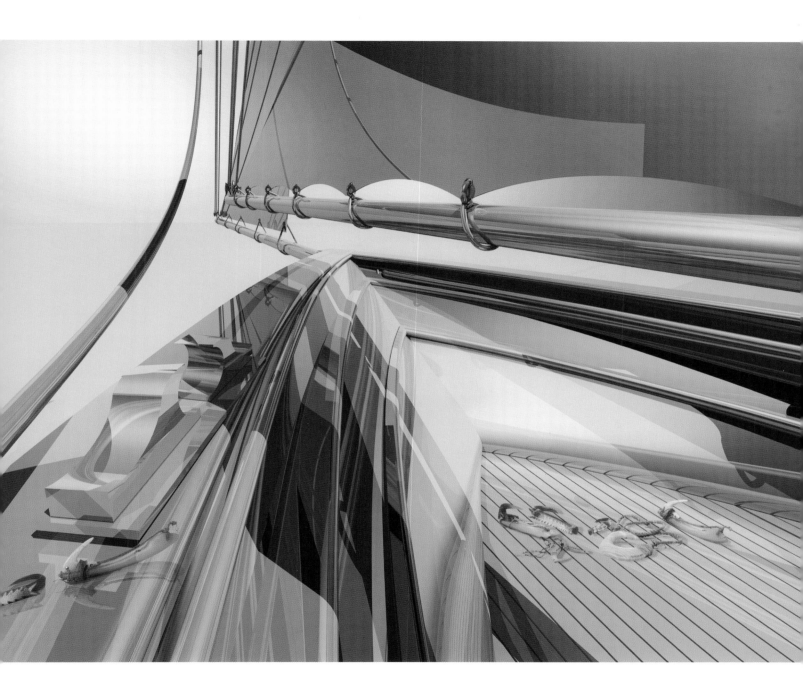

5   The Devil and the Medicine Box

The *Equator* reached Apemama in the Gilbert Islands in August 1889, then under the control of the tyrannical King Tembinok. Reluctantly, Tembinok offered the Stevenson party refuge, building a compound of huts for them which they named 'Equator Town'. The album photograph shows their daily living space, including hammocks and trunks taken from the schooner. The digital image incorporates a mother of pearl shell from The Writers' Museum. It sits in a fabricated medicine or devil-work box, gifted to Stevenson by a local wizard after he approached him seeking a cure for a cold.

Equator Town, Apemama, Gilbert Islands
Equator Album, The Writers' Museum, Edinburgh

The Presiding Genius

This work draws from a strange album photograph showing a trader's veranda with a figurehead rescued from a wreck. In the artwork the figure stands amongst some discarded mother of pearl shells, sent from Samoa by Stevenson to his cousin, Lady Kyllachy. The figurehead recalls a 'woman of exorbitant stature' who appears in Stevenson's tale, *The Ebb-Tide*. To its left, on the balcony, sits Stevenson's ring, embossed with the word TUSITALA, which translates from Samoan as 'teller of tales'.

Traders Verandah with Figurehead from Wreck, Penryn Islands
SS Janet Nicoll Album, The Writers' Museum, Edinburgh

7 The Feast of the Opening of the Road of the Loving Heart

Stevenson settled at Vailima, his home in Apia on the island of Upolu, Samoa. Here he continued to be involved in Samoan politics, visiting imprisoned tribal chiefs caught up in a civil war. The chiefs were released, and as a token of their gratitude they constructed a road up to Vailima for the Stevenson family. The album photograph shows a feast staged by Stevenson in honour of the road builders. The large wooden bowl was used to make kava, an intoxicating drink prepared from the roots of pepper plants and drunk at ceremonial occasions.

The Feast of the Opening of the Road of the Loving Heart, Vailima, Samoa
Samoan Album, The Writers' Museum, Edinburgh

8 Count Nerli Paints the Original Robert Louis Stevenson

In August 1892, the itinerant Italian artist, Girolamo Nerli, arrived in Apia and asked to paint a portrait of Stevenson, a self-confessed 'difficult subject'. Several copies of the painting survive in museums in Scotland and America, posing the question which one is the 'original'? Three versions of the Scottish National Portrait Gallery's portrait appear in this work – the hand painted object (and its various copies) becomes an infinitely reproducible digital surrogate. The clinical, alienating feel of the virtual interior contrasts markedly with the dramatic album photograph of Stevenson and his wife, Fanny, at home in their drawing room at Vailima.

Vailima, Samoa
Samoan Album, The Writers' Museum, Edinburgh

Laid in State

Stevenson died of a brain haemorrhage at his home in Vailima on the 3 December 1894; he was forty-four years old. His coffin, covered by the ensign from the yacht, *Casco*, was laid out for the people of Samoa to pay their last respects. The album photograph, taken by the commercial photographer, Thomas Andrew, is one of the most famous of the Stevenson family portraits. The digital work strips it of its human content, pointing to the sense of loss engendered by Stevenson's death. The *Casco's* ensign is now owned by The Speculative Society at the University of Edinburgh, of which Stevenson himself was once a member.

Vailima, Samoa
Samoan Album, The Writers' Museum, Edinburgh

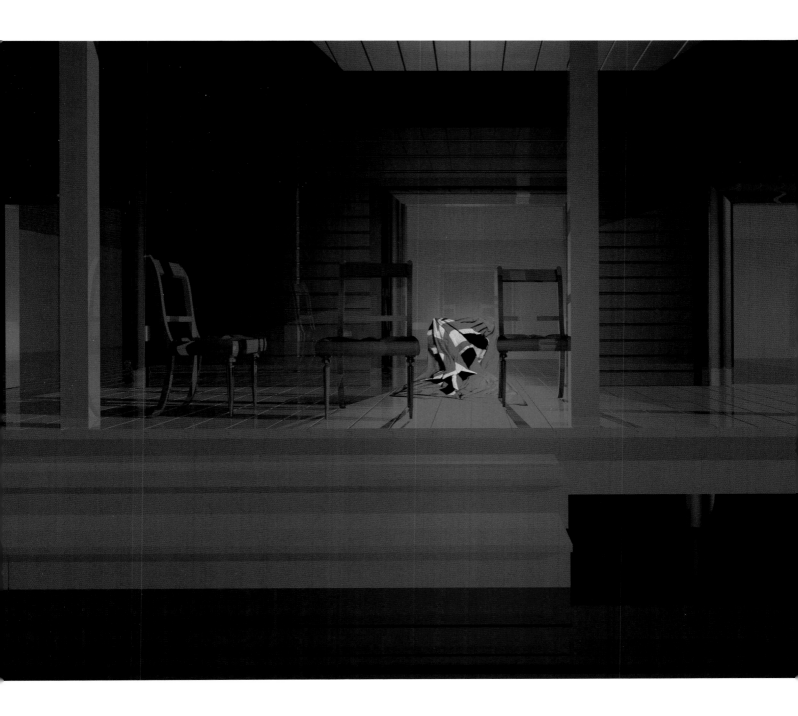

Explorations Between Image and Place

JAMES LAWSON

Encounters with the stories of others' lives can change our own. Once our imaginations are possessed by the story of a person's life, our own lives receive something of its impress, and, like narrative itself, acquire an intimation of the providential. When it is the life of a teller of stories that we come upon, we are called to follow, like the children of Hamlyn.

As an artist, Sara Gadd has consistently been drawn by the drama and pathos of other people's lives. At Craiglockart, in Edinburgh, the cases of First World War officers being treated for shell shock – most famously, Siegfried Sassoon and Wilfred Owen – inspired her photographic work, *Hydropathic*. In 1999, she travelled to the South Seas in the footsteps of her great-grandfather, who had been a missionary on the island of Samoa at the beginning of the twentieth century. There, she came upon Robert Louis Stevenson, in the form of a web of tales of the writer and adventurer who had sailed to several of the island groups of the Pacific, observed the curious scenes (all the while recalling his place of origin, Scotland and Britain) and died, in 1894, in Samoa, known as *Tusitala*, the 'teller of tales'. Stevenson has the power to detain, and has provoked Sara Gadd to create an account of his and her own experience in a series of nine images, created photographically and digitally, entitled *Navigating Stevenson*.

The attraction of Stevenson for Sara Gadd lies partly in her identification with the life of the traveller. On his several voyages, Stevenson lived, by definition, the dislocated life. His places of island habitation were temporary, just as impermanent and shifting as the world through which he passed. How to make sense of the perennially unfamiliar and ineluctably strange? Stevenson had a strategy – to live between memory and experience – the one anchoring reason and moral understanding, the other postponing judgemental attitude.

In making a sort of portrait or biography or narrative of Stevenson in the South Seas, Sara Gadd responds to her own sense of recognising him. The portrait, in the fullest sense, needs to emerge not just from the vision of the subject, but from an act of identification, empathy and imaginative assimilation. By her representational and constructional method, she offers not a record but a meditation upon Stevenson, the traveller. Past and present meet in the work.

The method is elaborate, technically painstaking and even a homage to dusty scholarship. There are two photographic stages in the process, and there are three computer stages. First, she makes copy-photographs of images in Stevenson family albums. She then constructs computer versions of the places represented. As family photographs, the scenes are often thronged with people.

As computer reconstructions of places, they are empty of animated incident. The other part of Sara Gadd's process is to select objects to inhabit the evacuated scenes. These are relics of Robert Louis Stevenson, preserved in museums. She photographs them and renders them into digital form, after which, using *Adobe Photoshop*, she sets them down in the places that she has constructed using *Microstation J*. At last, an image exists, one evoking a significant place in Stevenson's travels and containing a significant object. What had been isolated in album and museum are now recombined, in the computer's memory and in the image.

It is, therefore, in museum and archive that the raw material is collected, and in camera, darkroom and computer that it is processed into the final composite works. What results are settings, unmistakably created inside the computer, but also evocative of real places and occasions on Stevenson's travels. Here, the photographer (the specialist draughtsman with light) and the artist (the interpreter of experience) creates with the computer. Sara Gadd makes atmospherically richer environments than the relatively undeveloped photographic chemistry of Stevenson's age could achieve. In *Catching Fish off the Bowsprit of the Schooner 'Equator'* (plate 4), her own memory of the Pacific, together with her art, enable her to realise the drenching yellow light that blazes off the noon-time ship's deck and bleaches through the canvas of the sails. Her entitlement to expressive manipulation of the scene lets her, in *Laid in State* (plate 9), redden the light by which Stevenson's flag-draped coffin is illuminated. Similarly, *The Feast of the Opening of the Road of the Loving Heart* (plate 7) combines shadow, cast shadow, lustre and the grid of dim reflection to produce a richness of light effect that evokes time and place with mesmerising conviction.

Sara Gadd also observes an irony: it has been an act of dislocation to which museum and archive have been party. The theme is presented in *Count Nerli Paints the Original Robert Louis Stevenson* (plate 8). The painting, *Robert Louis Stevenson* by Nerli, is seen on the wall whilst its clones migrate, or vice versa. Of course, three Stevensons in the same space also put us in mind of the author's interest in dualism and the split personality, most famously in his story, *The Strange Case of Dr Jekyll and Mr Hyde*. Objects occupied contexts in Stevenson's life. They have now, in the museum, a final resting place beyond use and under glass. Moments, immortalised in the albums as snapshots, have, except to scholarship, been consigned to an archival oblivion or else, in these technologically advanced times, to the limbo of a digital database. Sara Gadd has sought permission for the cases to be unlocked and the leaves of the albums to be turned. She has made her photographs and now sets about the representation of another dislocation, for it was the condition of Stevenson's life that his objects appeared in a shifting scene. The objects were essentially mnemonic or talismanic – points of *durée* in a process of change, aids to experiential navigation. Now, they are fragile again, removed from the chill security of their museum cases. Delicate crockery will be lucky to survive being left on the ship's rail in *On Board the Yacht 'Casco', Stevenson Awaits the Arrival of Kooamua, Chief of Hatiheu, a Civilised Cannibal and the Last Eater of Long-pig* (plate 1). These plates provoke a shiver of horror in the context. The other relics will also be returned to scenes of 'object-peril'; the computer-generated places evoking the album images, in turn recording the occasion of peril, history itself – that so few objects have survived. The peril of sudden catastrophe – the remorselessness of fate – excited Stevenson. Markheim, in the story of that name (1886) says, 'Every second is a cliff, if you think of it – a cliff a mile high – high enough, if we fall, to dash us out of every feature of humanity.'

Combining objects and images in this way, Sara Gadd reminds us of the curious similarity that exists between relics and photographs. First, there is a reminder of the wonderment (so easy to forget) which is at the heart of photography – that, by the action of the photographer, the past has left a physical trace – frail to be sure, but proof of itself nonetheless. The thought is the stronger for its being set in the antithetical context of computer-generated space, something that is incapable of carrying any burden of proof. Then, from the stable context of the museum, the objects make a larger claim, but one that is, in essence, the same. They have the character of relics and they demand to be acknowledged as unbroken connections with specifics of the past. The more fragile, the luckier and the more remarkable. As threads, too, they are unbroken, despite distance of space and time. We hold onto the end of them; their integrity a matter of faith and hope.

Sara Gadd, with the aid of the computer, shifts the perspective and allows us to see them, we could say, 'side-on'. Supplying a historically-based scene, she provokes the historical imagination, which offers a way of looking at the venerable from this different angle; one where veneration ceases to be the appropriate attitude of mind. Thinking about the past historically is different from claiming connection with it. Whilst our aim in touching the relic is to be in contact with the unique actuality of its momentous existence in the past, historical thinking establishes no such density of actuality. It discovers instead the social, political or economic 'space' of the object; its context or, we could say, its drama.

Nothing is proved in this space; all is for interpretation and debate. The relic, on the contrary, is a thread of certainty.

The computer artist is not the first to create images addressing historical imagination in this way. The geometric perspective system that imaging computers use today was invented in the period of the Renaissance. With it, painters were able to create the illusion of rational spaces in which figures could move plausibly and seem to act autonomously. It may be said that space containing action is nothing less than history itself. It invites empathetic enquiry and pondered judgement. By contrast, the image that had the stilled character of a relic, making no acknowledgement of space and time, resisted evaluation in terms of morality and truth: these, instead, were absolutes. It is the person who lives outside of the security of dogma – the moral wayfarer – who takes courage to negotiate the uncertainties of context, of historical space – that of Renaissance art and the computer.

When photography was invented, what was it to be used for – authenticating banknotes, providing models for lacemakers to copy, documenting criminals? The same sort of question can be asked of the computer. It too is multifunctional. But, as the camera fell into the hands of the photographers, Hill and Adamson, Carleton Watkins and André Kertész, it acquired a prestigious use. The computer now falls into the hands of the computer artist. Sara Gadd, creating contexts, follows such Renaissance artists as Filippo Brunelleschi and Piero della Francesca, and tells us what the computer can be – a humanist device.

What she creates inside the computer are advisedly 'places' rather than views. And for all their dependency on photographs and their superficial resemblance to photographic imagery, they are to be distinguished sharply from the product of the camera. In fact, the photograph is also to be distinguished from the product of the Renaissance perspective system. The essential difference is that the painted setting and the computer-generated place are constructed, whereas, instead of constructing the scene, the camera observes it. The prominence of lens-based media has implanted an idea that has been very tenacious since the invention of photography (though admittedly one encouraged by the painterly tradition within Western painting) – that the eye is 'outside' of what it looks at. In fact, it is only sometimes the case: for example, it is untrue of our vision as we move through space. It is also untrue of Renaissance perspective and computer-generated spaces. Only in the absence of a constructive mentality with regard to these spaces is the observer a viewer upon it, rather than its occupant. To put the matter another way, the minds of the artist and the viewer are, because of the rational coherency of the depicted space, 'inside' the space that it constructs.

Significantly, the places or contexts that Sara Gadd makes for the objects of Stevenson's life in the South Seas do not include Stevenson himself. The partial exceptions are the last two images of the series, where Stevenson is before us in the form of Nerli's portrait and the last where his presence as a corpse in a coffin is to be inferred. By creating the places rather than imitating the populated scenes of the album photographs, Sara Gadd stands not where the camera was, but inside the place that the computer constructs – that is, one like the place that Stevenson inhabited. It is he, as well as she and we, who look upon the scenes. We possess his eyes as we come upon the objects of familiar use within his dislocated experience, or objects scarce acknowledged perhaps, but destined to survive him.

A Vitalised Museum

CATHERINE MORIARTY

I sat … in the midst of a museum of strange objects – paddles, and battle-clubs, and baskets, rough-hewn stone images, ornaments of threaded shell, cocoanut [sic] bowls, snowy cocoanut plumes – evidences and examples of another earth, another climate, another race, and another (if a ruder) culture.[1]

Robert Louis Stevenson was of distinct appearance and those who met him commented upon it. His physique, his clothing, his demeanour all provoked discussion – he was described in letters, press reports, diaries and journals. Artists who made visual portraits of Stevenson attempted to create a likeness in either two or three dimensions that satisfied the expectations of those who knew the writer well and those who had read about him. John Singer Sargent's canvases of the mid-1880s, two of which survive, are famous painted examples. So is Count Nerli's enigmatic head and shoulders study of 1892 which Stevenson's wife, Fanny, felt had failed to convey the character of her husband. Sculpted portraits include the bronze relief in the High Kirk of St Giles, Edinburgh, by the American sculptor Augustus St Gaudens, a work of which Stevenson approved – he is depicted in profile, in bed, at work – and considered to be a 'speaking likeness'. David Watson Stevenson sculpted a marble bust, which is now displayed at the Scottish National Portrait Gallery, Edinburgh and a bronze statue that stands in the entrance to Kelvingrove Art Gallery and Museum in Glasgow. Photographic portraits were the result of sittings in commercial studios or the work of friends and family. The wide publication of these images over the years, and more recently their ready distribution by electronic means, has made the appearance of Stevenson familiar.

As Robert Louis Stevenson knew so well, portraits need not be like-nesses in a conventional sense. A portrait can emerge from a person's possessions, for the objects owned by an individual have a remarkable power to animate them in their absence, be it temporary or perma-nent, recent or many years past. Archaeologists know this well despite the often greater distance of their subjects in terms of time and their frequent anonymity. Stevenson was enthralled by the imagining that the remnant possessions of others pro-voked.

In *Treasure Island* Stevenson describes Jim and his mother search-ing through the captain's sea chest. As they hunt for the gold the dead pirate owed the family, Jim finds the bundle of papers that include the fateful map. As they look through the contents of the chest, the life of their owner is played over. Among numer-ous souvenirs of the pirate's experi-ences they find, 'an old boat-cloak whitened with sea salt on many a harbour bar' and West Indian sea-shells. Jim comments, 'it has often set me thinking since that he should have carried about these shells with him in his wandering, guilty and hunted life'. Stevenson uses these objects to evoke the life and character of their owner and in death they become relics, certainly soon to be dispersed, but for this moment united by their common ownership.

Though writers leave a legacy in their texts, we read reproductions. It is the original manuscript that evokes an aura, conveying the labour of the writer in the act of creating – we imagine the movement of pen on paper. Yet objects other than texts may provoke our speculations. At The Writers' Museum in Edinburgh, possessions that Stevenson owned are arranged in display cases. They include items he kept on or near his person (his pipe, his cigarette papers, his riding boots), and items that occupied the space around him and represent his relations with others (a plate from the dining set at Vailima scratched from so much use, a wine glass, grass fans, shells he sent as a souvenir, fishing hooks and a Kava bowl which was passed among visitors and the visited). Yet in the display case of the museum they are distanced from their original owner and context in both time and space. Similarly, a cabinet of curiosities, or even mundane accumulations of things, evoke the presence of the individual who assembled the collection. The life of this person is the invisible matrix that connects the items on display. As Stevenson's descriptions of objects 'vitalise' the inanimate, so the spectator in the museum attempts to imagine the original owner sipping from the glass, lighting his pipe or stooping to pick up a shell from a Pacific beach. The biography of the object and that of its owner coincide. Though during the life of the latter this may have been for a brief moment, in the display case of the museum this relationship is ossified.

Yet we have some visual guidance as to the spaces occupied by Stevenson and the objects in their original context. Stevenson and his family photographed their journeying to the South Seas, their time in Samoa and their voyages to other islands. Pasted into albums, sepia prints evoke sequentially the strange bohemian lifestyle of Stevenson and his family and their interactions with the local islanders. Reproductions of a selection of these photographs – the albums safe in the museum store – are framed around the walls of the Writers' Museum with the objects displayed below them. The museum visitor attempts to connect the relics of Stevenson's presence with the images of their owner and context. Exhibited in the museum we are convinced of their authenticity.

Other Stevenson material is located around the world at the places where the writer lived or visited, at Monterey and Silverado in California, in Samoa itself, or at institutions that have subsequently acquired writings or objects. While scholars and enthusiasts have known for years of this global collection – indeed the stakeholders in Stevenson's life have long been international – it is the ready distribution of this data by electronic means that allows the geographical distances seemingly to collapse. The global dispersal of Stevenson's material legacy is now readily connected by digital replication.

Sara Gadd's images ask us to consider how the spatial relations of the museum appear to alter through the use of digital technology. Digital copies of original photographs and objects may lead a new and different life beyond the walls of the museum. It is now possible to rejoin or relocate, even repatriate virtually these separate parts. While museum artefacts were always available for reproduction, this was limited by curatorial discretion. Now digital images, published on the world wide web, may be accessed either deliberately or serendipitously, in sequence, or in isolation; they may retain or lose their relations to each other. Museum custodians publish digital data in the name of research and scholarship with the aim of expanding audiences and contributing to the cultural wealth and integrity of remote resources. The use that is made of this material is in part known, but also, and significantly, unknown.

If the contents of a collection can be re- or dis-assembled, transferred to different contexts, placed in new arrangements, modified or enhanced, the curatorial authority to order and present is upended, indeed potentially subverted. Representations of the objects are now 'out of place'. Their use and meaning is no longer prescribed, defying the conventions

of museum and archival practice. Yet the originals remain safe and sound, in their tissue-wrapped album, their acid-free box, their climatically controlled display case.

Sara Gadd's work examines how a photograph of an original context may be simulated in a digital format and an image of an authentic object, digitally replicated, may be joined with it to create a new image. Though the tradition of montage is a long one, now the immediate appearance may be seamless and perhaps, in some contexts, disturbingly so. Technologies that enable the origins of the components to become less clear facilitate 'cut and paste' of a high order. Gadd's project explores these capabilities and their potential in the creation of representational meaning. In digital contexts the ability to manipulate images has escalated, as have the number of people with access to this technology. Spectators will adjust to reading new kinds of assemblages, requiring us to reconsider issues of authenticity. As the digital copy is copied and re-copied, this chain of replication moves it further away from the original with its direct connection to the subject. Its relationship to the parent object becomes ambiguous. If a painted or sculpted portrait is the result of sittings with the subject, or made posthumously from photographs, does this affect our response to it? Does the presence of the subject seem diluted through reproduction or has this long been an illusion instilled by the museum, the collector and the connoisseur?

Inevitably, manipulation of this kind provokes anxiety. Not only by unsettling the expectations of the viewer, but also directly through the transformations, additions and omissions it makes possible. The objects and spaces presented in Sara Gadd's works are disturbing, deliberately so, without their owner and the family, the friends and associates that animated them. For Stevenson, while interested in the ability of objects to evoke the absent, was primarily concerned with relations between the living. These depopulated spaces recall stage sets where the cast has walked-off or, more chillingly, massacres where every inhabitant has been killed. What is left to us, the material traces of a life, whether authentic or simulated, emphasises the absence of the personality that gave them meaning. While texts live on in different formats and languages they possess vivacity. They may be abridged or translated, yet they have a life independent of their creator. Indeed, Stevenson was a master of fictions, of making the implausible believable.

Examining digital surrogates and reconstructions, we enquire of the source, we assume it has some connection to a tangible reality. Not simply a habit of attribution we need to check, for we still treat the representation before us as a photograph, rather than as a very different kind of image. We find ourselves asking, as people have done for so long with conventional portraiture, how alike is the likeness?

Therein were cables, windlasses and blocks of every size and capacity; cabin windows and ladders; rusty tanks, a companion hutch; a binnacle with its brass mountings and its compass idly pointing, in the confusion and dust of that shed, to a forgotten pole; ropes, anchors, harpoons, a blubber dipper of copper, green with years, a steering wheel, a tool chest with the vessel's name upon the top, the Asia: *a whole curiosity shop of sea curios, gross and solid, heavy to lift, ill to break, bound with brass and shod with iron. Two wrecks at the least must have contributed to this random heap of lumber; and as Herrick looked upon it, it seemed to him as if the ships' companies were there on guard, and he heard the tread of feet and whisperings, and saw with the tail of his eye the commonplace ghosts of sailor men.*[2]

1. Robert Louis Stevenson and Lloyd Osbourne, *The Wrecker*, Edinburgh, 1996, p.108 (1st edn 1892).

2. Robert Louis Stevenson and Lloyd Osbourne, *The Ebb-Tide*, Edinburgh, 1996, p.87 (1st edn 1894).

Robert Louis Stevenson

Sara Gadd

1850   Born on 13 November

1866   Writes *The Pentland Rising, a Page of History, 1666*, which is published anonymously

1867   Begins classes in engineering and science

1871   Tells father of intention to abandon engineering. Starts reading law at The University of Edinburgh

1872   Passes preliminary examination for Scottish Bar

1873   Visits England and France, but too ill to try for entrance into English law. *Roads* published

1875   Is called to the Scottish Bar as an advocate

1676   Meets Mrs Fanny van de Grift Osbourne

1878   First book published, *An Inland Voyage*

1880   Marries Fanny on 19 May

1881   Visits Braemar where he begins *Treasure Island*

1883   *Treasure Island* is published in book form

1885   *A Child's Garden of Verses* is published and starts writing *Kidnapped*

1886   *The Strange Case of Dr Jekyll and Mr Hyde* is published

1887   Last visit to Edinburgh – sails to America

1888   Cruise to the islands of South Seas

1889   Purchases land near Apia (capital of Samoa) and builds Pineapple Cottage. Publishes *The Master of Ballantrae*

1890   Begins building his home at Vailima

1892   Starts writing *Weir of Hermiston* and *St Ives*

1894   Robert Louis Stevenson dies on 3 December and is buried on top of Vaea Mountain

Sara Gadd is an artist and photography lecturer at Falmouth College of Arts. In 1999 she received a Winston Churchill Memorial Trust Fellowship allowing her to photograph in Samoa. Her subsequent exhibitions, *Navigators I* and *Navigators II: Home* were exhibited in Brighton in 2000 and 2001. In 2000 she was appointed Fellow in Photography and Digital Imaging at Napier University in Edinburgh, during which time she began work on *Navigating Stevenson*. Another project, *Hydropathic*, based on the history of the military hospital at Craiglockhart, Edinburgh was published in 2001. Sara Gadd exhibits her work widely and has won numerous awards and residencies.

Further Reading

Casey Blanton (ed.), *Picturing Paradise: Colonial Photography of Samoa, 1875 to 1925*, Southeast Museum of Photography, Daytona, 1995

Jenni Calder, *RLS: A Life Study*, London, 1980

Jenni Calder (ed.), *Stevenson and Victorian Scotland*, Edinburgh, 1981

Elizabeth Edwards, *Raw Histories: Photographs, Anthropology and Museums*, Oxford, 2001

Lev Manovich, *The Language of New Media*, Cambridge, Massachusetts and London, 2001

Edward Said, *Culture and Imperialism*, London, 1994

Ingrid Schaffner and Matthias Winzen (eds.), *Deep Storage: Collecting, Storing, and Archiving in Art*, Munich and New York, 1998

Robert Louis Stevenson, *A Footnote in History: Eight Years of Trouble in Samoa*, London, 1892

Robert Louis Stevenson, *Island Landfalls: Reflections from the South Seas*, Edinburgh, 1987

Robert Louis Stevenson, *The Letters of Robert Louis Stevenson*, Bradford A. Booth and Ernest Mehew (eds.), 8 vols., New Haven and London, 1994–5

Robert Louis Stevenson, *Tales of the South Seas*, Edinburgh, 1996

Robert Louis Stevenson, *In the South Seas*, London, 1998

Robert Louis Stevenson, *South Seas Tales*, Oxford, 1999

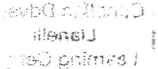

Websites

National Library of Scotland at: www.nls.uk/rlstevenson/index.html
Robert Louis Stevenson at: wwwesterni.unibg.it/siti_esterni/rls/rls.htm
Sara Gadd at: www.saragadd.com
Scottish Cultural Resources Network at: www.scran.ac.uk